YOUNG

AT ART

1996 - 1997

~~Grand View~~

Chairpersons: Lynn Hedani

Beth Lee

deleted

AMERICAN WATERCOLORS

AMERICAN WATERCOLORS

KATE F. JENNINGS

Crescent Books

New York/Avenel, New Jersey

This 1995 edition published by Crescent Books,
distributed by Random House Value Publishing, Inc.,
40 Engelhard Avenue,
Avenel, New Jersey 07001

Random House
New York Toronto · London · Sydney · Auckland

Produced by Brompton Books Corporation,
15 Sherwood Place,
Greenwich, Connecticut 06830

ISBN 0-517-12081-X

8 7 6 5 4 3 2 1

Printed and bound in China

PAGE 1
John La Farge
Wild Roses in an Antique Chinese Bowl, 1880
Watercolor on paper, 8½ × 7½ inches
Courtesy of Museum of Fine Arts, Boston, MA, bequest of
Elizabeth Howard Bartol (27.96)

PAGE 2
Jackson Pollock
Pattern, c.1945
Watercolor, brush and ink, pen and ink and gouache on paper,
22½ × 5½ inches (irregular)
Hirshhorn Museum and Sculpture Garden, Smithsonian
Institution, gift of the Joseph H. Hirshhorn Foundation, 1066
(66.4086)

PAGE 5
John Singer Sargent
Muddy Alligators, 1917
Watercolor over graphite on medium, textured cream wove paper
Worcester Art Museum, Worcester, MA, Sustaining Membership
Fund (1917.86)

CONTENTS

INTRODUCTION 6

WATERCOLOR'S BEGINNINGS 24

IMPRESSIONISM 38

MASTER REALISTS 56

MODERNISM ARRIVES 82

CONTEMPORARY AND ABSTRACT WATERCOLORS 102

ACKNOWLEDGMENTS 112

INTRODUCTION

The unique properties of the watercolor medium make it ideally suited to the American temperament. It is easily transportable, its materials are relatively inexpensive, and its singular effects are quickly achieved and produce spontaneous, often accidental evocations of mood.

During the last 100 years, many of the finest watercolorists recognized internationally have been American, led by Winslow Homer, John Singer Sargent and Thomas Eakins, and followed by more modern stylists such as Edward Hopper, John Marin, Charles Burchfield, Charles Demuth and Georgia O'Keeffe. Their works are the products of creative individuals who adapted the unpredictable, improvisational nature of the watercolor medium to subjects, settings and concepts that typify the American experience and cultural influences.

America's strong commercial ties and close intellectual exchange with Great Britain during the nineteenth century fostered the development of established standards and techniques for the watercolor medium. Many of the earliest American practitioners were either born in England or derived their educational and artistic framework from English artists and critics. The finest watercolor papers of the nineteenth and early twentieth centuries often bear the watermark of J Whatman, a British manufacturer, while the Winsor and Newton water-soluble pigments, produced in readily-transportable tubes, were imported from England to stores in Philadelphia, Boston and New York in the early 1800s.

In 1840, Frederick Catherwood, a British artist, brought more than 500 drawings and watercolors from England to the United States, introducing the acknowledged British watercolor master J M W Turner to the American public. The British writer and art theoretician John Ruskin published a variety of articles and tracts promoting the medium, which were widely distributed in the United States in the mid-1800s and helped to popularize the Pre-Raphaelite style. This movement was dedicated to direct observation of nature, exactness of detail, meticulous brushwork, and delicate, jewel-like hues created by layers of transparent washes.

The development of the watercolor medium during the Victoria era, from 1820 to 1880, closely paralleled the ascendancy of the Hudson River School of painters, centered on New York City. Landscape scenes glorified the natural wonders of the region, and engineering feats such as bridges and canals were frequently featured to underscore America's commercial prominence. William Guy Wall, a British native, arrived in the United States in 1817 as a fully trained watercolorist. His most valuable contribution to the burgeoning interest in the medium was a series of engravings called the *Hudson River Port-folio*, which focused on local vistas and views of the bay of New York, the falls of the Passaic River, and the geography surrounding Fishkill, New York. These images were published in several editions from 1820 to 1828. Closely aligned to topographical maps of the region, they were factual renderings of specific places that required reportorial skills and a tight, realistic technique. Wall used a large brush to describe the sky and mountains, while finer brushwork denoted the figures and foliage in the foreground. Washes layered in hues of blue, green and brown predominated, laid down over pencil outlines.

The prints of William Guy Wall were highly popular, widely disseminated and frequently copied, and his watercolor paintings were exhibited in gallery shows in New York alongside oil paintings by the prominent Hudson River school artists, Frederic E Church and Asher B Durand. Wall was one of the fifteen founding members of the National Academy of Design, and in 1850 Wall, together with John William Hill, William Trost Richards and several other respected watercolor painters, established the New York Water Color Society, which staged America's first important exhibitions of watercolors at the

6

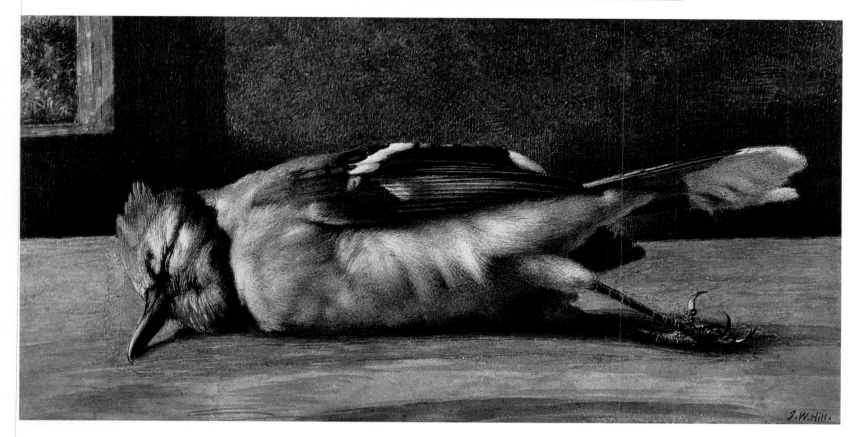

LEFT: Asher B. Durand's calling card, *c.* 1869, with his self-portrait (Metropolitan Museum of Art, New York, David Hunter McAlpin Fund, 1952, 52.605)

ABOVE: *Dead Blue Jay* by John William Hill, not dated, watercolor on paper (mounted on cardboard), 14¼ × 19¼ inches (Collection of the New-York Historical Society, NYC 1957.94)

Crystal Palace in New York in 1853. Landscape was the most prevalent subject and Turnersque skies in luminous, pellucid washes of yellow, rose and pale blue tints were in abundance.

John William Hill, another noted Victorian watercolorist, was also born in England, moved to Philadelphia in 1819, and arrived in New York in 1823. Trained by his father, an etcher and engraver, Hill assisted in the production of the aquatints for the *Hudson River Portfolio*. His early watercolor landscapes of the Erie Canal and his lithographs of upstate New York were stylistically akin to Wall's. He is best known for his later works, detailed studies of plants and birds which disclose his affinity for the artistic philosophy of John Ruskin. Ruskin believed that watercolor represented an advanced drawing technique, which could record nature truthfully and meticulously in natural settings with the addition of brilliant color. He promoted a technique know as stippling, the application of hundreds of tiny dots and brushstrokes, laid tightly together to intensify detail and create *trompe l'oeil* illusions. Ruskin's essay *The Elements of Drawing*, published in 1857, also implored artists to be sensitive to color effects:

You ought to love colour and to think nothing quite beautiful or perfect without it . . . Every hue is altered by every touch you add in other places.

Hill's studies of a branch of blossoms, a bird's nest or a twig of berries reflected a search for the universal truths that, like Ruskin, he believed could be discovered in nature. His water-

color still-life *Dead Blue Jay* possesses the almost photographic exactitude, tiny, stippled strokes, and delicate hues that typify Ruskin's Pre-Raphaelite followers in America. These artists banded together in New York in 1860 to form the Association for the Advancement of Truth in Art.

William Trost Richards was born in Philadelphia in 1833 and attended the Pennsylvania Academy of Art there. The precise style and degree of finish in the sea-coast scenes and marine paintings he began to produce in the 1860s disclose the attentiveness typical of Ruskin's disciples. Richards traveled to Europe on several occasions, and a dramatic storm encountered during a voyage to the Continent in 1867 inspired his fascination for the sea. The views he produced during summer pilgrimages to Atlantic City and Newport celebrate the ocean's beauty in all weathers and seasons. As well as providing an astonishing degree of geographical and botanical detail, Richards evoked the mesmerizing effects of mist and clouds by the sea, and conveyed with extraordinary accuracy the advance of waves along the shore. He achieved such verisimilitude by careful observation, as his son noted:

He stood for hours in the early days of Atlantic City or Cape May, with folded arms, studying the motion of the sea, until people thought him insane.

Richards worked on a large scale, often creating works approximately two foot by three foot, to vie with the oil paintings then currently displayed. His watercolors were critically acclaimed and actively collected and he won many awards, including medals at the 1876 Centennial Exhibition and, in 1905, the Pennsylvania Academy's Gold Medal of Honor. George Whitney, a wealthy Philadelphia manufacturer, amassed 275 watercolors by Richards. Another 85 were collected by the Reverend Elias Magoon of New York, who later gave a selection to Vassar College. Magoon also donated 54 paintings to the Metropolitan Museum in 1880 in an effort to

match the bequest of J M W Turner's watercolors made to London's Tate Gallery.

Another important watercolorist from Philadelphia was Thomas Moran, who was born in Lancashire, England, in 1837 and settled in Pennsylvania in 1844. After an apprenticeship at a wood engraving firm, and a limited artistic training with the marine painter James Hamilton, Moran returned to England, where he studied the works of Turner. The results of his journey are apparent in the marvelous atmospheric effects and breathtaking grandeur of Moran's watercolors of the American West.

In 1871 Moran was enlisted as the staff artist for Ferdinand Hayden's expedition to the Yellowstone region. In the course of eight journeys, Moran made numerous sketches, watercolors and oil paintings of the Colorado River, the Grand Canyon, Yosemite, Lake Tahoe, the Tetons and various sites in New Mexico. Watercolor was particularly adaptable to the demands of travelling out West in relatively primitive conditions. Moran's copious illustrations romanticizing the physical glories of these vast territories helped to persuade Congress to establish the Yellowstone region as America's first national park. In his paintings Moran establishes the monumentality and the daunting emotional impact of precipitous mountains and vibrant buttes by a linear underpinning that draws the eye into the distant horizon, furnishing a composition that asserts geographical scope. Special rock formations are carefully rendered to attract attention, while others blur and coalesce into the background setting. These panoramic scenes, devoid of any human presence, have an otherworldly, almost religous, aura.

Moran's rich bronze, copper and blue hues, the tinted papers he employed, and his steamy, hazy cloud formations are clearly derived from Turner's techniques. A series of 15 of his Yellowstone watercolors were reproduced as chromolithographs by Prang and Company of Boston in 1876. Thomas Moran's scintillating watercolors were proof of his dictum:

An artist's business is to produce for the spectator of his picture the impression produced by nature on himself.

During the 1860s and 1870s watercolor painting gained increasing respectability and visibility, due in large part to the establishment in 1866 of the American Society of Painters in Watercolors. Its shows coincided with the regular exhibition schedule at the National Academy of Design in New York. Its membership, which soon included William Trost Richards,

LEFT ABOVE: *Harbor* by Alfred Thompson Bricher, late 1880s, watercolor heightened with white, 14½ × 20⅞6 inches (The Brooklyn Museum, NY, gift of Mrs Allison Clement Withers in memory of Grace Graef Clement, 52.58)

LEFT BELOW: Eakins in his Chestnut Studio, photographer unknown.

BELOW: *The Gates of the Hudson* by Jasper Francis Cropsey, 1891, watercolor over graphite on paper, 17¾ × 26¾ inches (The Fine Arts Museums of San Francisco, Achenbach Foundation for Graphic Arts, gift of Henry F. Dickinson to the M.H. de Young Museum)

Thomas Moran, John William Hill and his son John Henry Hill, Winslow Homer and Thomas Eakins, attracted significant attention from America's most notable art patrons, such as Thomas B Clarke, the first president of the Metropolitan Museum, William T Evans, and Charles Lang Freer, whose gallery is now associated with the Smithsonian in Washington, DC. In 1969 a valuable text by the art theorist A F Bellows called *Water Color Painting: Some Facts and Authorities in Relation to its Durability* proclaimed:

. . . For certain luminous qualities, for purity of tint and tone, for delicate gradations, especially in skies and distances, watercolor has decided advantages over oil.

In addition, the relatively low prices for watercolors, from only $30 or $40 for lesser known artists to $125 to $250 for Winslow Homer's early works, made the medium accessible to the general American public as well as to wealthy collectors.

In 1873 the Society held the largest and most popular exhibition of watercolors by foreign and native artists yet seen in the United States. This event had a significant impact, noted by the art historian, Helen A Cooper, who wrote:

By establishing beyond question watercolor as a serious medium, it gave a tremendous impetus to the cause of watercolor painting in America.

By the time of the centennial celebrations in 1876, America's interest in landscape themes was lessening and the art market began to favor instead depictions of the human

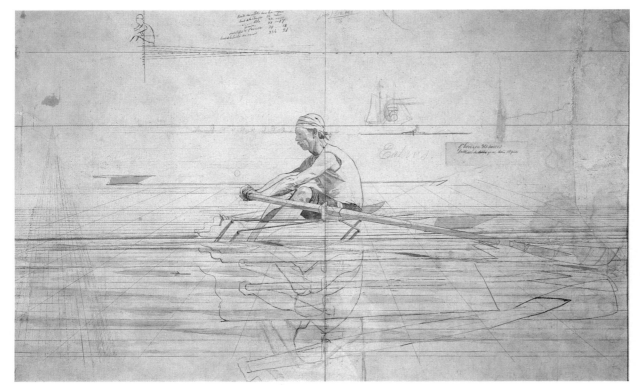

figure, genre scenes of everyday life and sporting events, and realistic portraiture. Thomas Eakins, born in Philadelphia in 1844, had a classical academic background, and adopted an intellectual approach to the human form that made his portraits singular expressions of technical refinement and absorbing psychological studies of character. Eakins received his early artistic training at the Pennsylvania Academy of Fine Arts, where he was required to make endless drawings from plaster casts as well as from the model. To further satisfy his scientific interest in anatomy, Eakins enrolled in additional classes at the Jefferson Medical College. He later went to Paris to study at the Ecole des Beaux Arts. During his four years in Europe he developed a particular interest in the works of Rembrandt and Diego Velásquez, both masters of portraiture technique.

Returning to Philadelphia, Eakins devoted his painting and photographic skills to local subjects, particularly athletes engaged in competitive contests and probing, meditative portraits of his family and friends. His watercolors represented only a small fraction of his oeuvre, consisting of just 30 or so works, completed early in his career during the 1870s and early 1880s. However, his painstaking, judiciously wrought work presages later realistic watercolorists, and reveals a scientific interest in the effects of light on form which is most successfully attained in the medium of watercolor.

For recreation, Eakins rowed a single scull on the Schuylkill River and he became fascinated with the figure of John Biglin, a professional oarsman who frequented the river. In preparation for his watercolor of Biglin, Eakins embarked on a large-scale, perspective study of the rower which shows his exact approach to problems of three dimensions. In the finished watercolor, Eakins ignores the fluid properties of the medium, preferring densely grouped flecks of paint to establish surfaces and shadows. One of Eakin's characteristic stylistic devices was to place the heads of his characters near the horizon line, or a major horizontal element in the background, to focus the viewer's attention. He further accentuates Biglin's head with a red bandana, the only spot of bright color in the painting. The figure of Biglin thereby achieves an almost static solidity that is rather unusual for watercolor studies. The pose of the rower leaning forward for the stroke adds an element of tension, and provides an excuse to explore the musculature of a body in action.

The finished watercolor (page 34) was hung at the 1874 exhibition of the American Society of Painters in Watercolor, and Eakins became a regular exhibitor, whose works were critically acclaimed and well-liked by the public. A typical American Victorian, Eakins combined a spirit of scientific inquiry with a certain moral rectitude and poetic delight in indigenous American characters and scenes. His watercolors were created at a time when the Watercolor Society was reaching its peak of popularity. By 1880, huge, lavish catalogs of the annual show were produced, including reproductions of over 800 paintings displayed that year.

Another nineteenth-century artist skilled in rendering the human figure was Winslow Homer, now acclaimed as the greatest watercolorist America has yet produced. Born in Boston in 1836, Homer's early portrait studies exhibit the draftsmanship he learned as an apprentice lithographer at J H Bufford and Sons in Boston. In his role as an illustrator for magazines such as *Harper's Weekly*, *Appleton's Journal* and *Every Saturday*, Homer developed strong, clear outlines, bold contrasts of light and dark, and simplified details in his watercolor sketches that could readily be adapted to woodblock carvings for reproduction purposes.

In subject matter and stylistic references, Homer's early watercolor figures fit squarely within the Victorian vernacular. A sentimental mood of quiet reverie pervades the pose of a young girl reading in *The New Novel*, and youthful exuberance and boyish escapades are depicted in *Sailing the Catboat* and *Three Boys on the Shore*. Homespun charm and childhood innocence are evoked in Homer's rustic settings, gingham dresses and straw hats. These images paralleled popular literature of the era, especially Louisa May Alcott's *Little Women* of 1868 and Mark Twain's *Tom Sawyer* of 1876. The provincial mood of Homer's early watercolor subjects did not, however, appeal to more worldly, cosmopolitan critics, most notable of whom was the expatriate American author, Henry James, then residing in London. James remarked of Homer's scenes on view at the Watercolor Society's annual show:

We detest his subjects . . . little barefoot urchins and little girls in calico sunbonnets . . . Mr Homer is almost barbarously simple . . . He has chosen the least pictorial features of the least pictorial range of scenery and civilization; he has resolutely treated them as if they *were* pictorial, as if they were every inch as good as Capri and Tangiers.

Following the example of expatriates such as James, members of America's upper classes and artistic coteries embarked in the last two decades of the nineteenth century on pilgrimages to Europe. Even Homer was lured to Cullercoates, in northern England, to discover new material and techniques for his watercolors, which did not reach the height of their originality or command of the medium for another decade or so. America's elite sought the cultural sophistication and elegant, old-world refinement cultivated in Continental drawing rooms, historic palaces and museums, and salon soirées in Paris, London, Venice and Rome. Several talented American artists accompanied these wealthy connoisseurs in search of both classical training and the subtle polish and patronage associated with European social circles.

Chief among these artists was James Abbott McNeill Whistler. Born in 1834 into a strictly religious household in Lowell, Massachusetts, Whistler attended West Point before abandoning the military at 21 and fleeing to Europe to pursue a career in the arts. In Paris he developed friendships with younger artists such as Henri Fantin-Latour, Gustave Courbet,

Edgar Degas, Edouard Manet and Claude Monet. He was among the first Americans to embrace the tenets of Impressionism. Whistler's own style was suggestive rather than descriptive, dedicated to capturing the delicate moods of nature with an economy of detail and simplicity of color. He influenced the direction of American artists toward subjective, expressive and poetic vistas with his small, calligraphic seascapes, urban views, genre scenes and figure studies. His manner was almost minimalist, painting wet into wet with the surface of the page already saturated, over which liquid washes were applied and then casually blotted to achieve the effect of a 'controled accident.' Whistler also made frequent allusions to music in the titles of his watercolors, calling them 'nocturnes,' 'harmonies' and 'notes.'

Whistler left Paris in 1859 for London, where he lived in Chelsea, close to the River Thames. His fluid, effervescent technique so offended the Pre-Raphaelite critic John Ruskin that the latter publicly described Whistler's work as little more than 'flinging a pot of paint in the public's face.' In response, Whistler filed a libel suit against Ruskin which proved disastrously expensive, and fruitless; he was awarded a farthing in settlement. He fled to Venice in the late 1870s to recoup his reputation and career. There he explored the canals, in a gondola fitted with his watercolor supplies, and began a memorable series of sketches loaded with water effects and soft, hazy light. His formats were emphatically horizontal, little more than sea

and sky reduced to essentials, a characteristic of the Japanese prints by artists such as Hiroshige which interested him. He traveled to Amsterdam and later returned to England, continuing his abbreviated, sensitive impressions of beaches, piers and riversides, which offer a surprising feeling of aerial perspective on flat sheets rarely larger than 8 by 10 inches.

The luminous hues and reductive linear elements of Oriental art were also absorbed by John La Farge, who employed its idioms with particular finesse in his floral still lifes. The son of wealthy French emigré parents, La Farge was born in New York City in 1835 and raised in Newport, Rhode Island. After graduating from college, he studied the Old Masters in Paris in the studio of Thomas Couture. On his return to America, his services became much in demand for neoclassical murals and stained glass commissions, for which he prepared extensive preliminary sketches in watercolor.

La Farge discovered beauty in the commonplace, such as a simple Chinese bowl filled with roses, whose fragile petals seemed so translucent in La Farge's painting that a critic claimed they appeared 'made of a breath or a blush.' He made use of the white of the watercolor page for highlights in the blossoms and bowl, and evoked background depth with multiple layers of washes he identified as 'veilings and sequences,' borrowed from the Japanese prints he collected. An advocate of the French Barbizon style, La Farge was no doubt exposed to the work of the Impressionists Monet and Pissarro through the efforts of the French dealer, Paul Durand-Ruel, who brought more than 300 Barbizon and Impressionist paintings to New York for display in 1886.

The *plein-air* sketches La Farge produced of the Newport

ABOVE: *Little Scheveningen: Gray Note* by James McNeill Whistler, 1890s, watercolor on paper, 5 × 8½ inches (Courtesy of Museum of Fine Arts, Boston, MA, gift of Walter Gay, 23.251)

BELOW: Maurice Prendergast.

BELOW RIGHT: *Sunrise in Fog over Kyoto* by John La Farge, 1886, watercolor on paper, 7⅛ × 11¾ inches (The Currier Gallery of Art, Manchester, NH, gift of Clement S Houghton, 1948.5)

seashore have the spontaneous, unpretentious contours, and the sense of wonder at the powers of nature, associated with the Impressionists. In *Moonlit Seascape* he allowed passages of white pigment to pool and float, illuminating the clouds, and freely blotted deeper blues on the surface of the ocean to convey a mood of immediacy. When La Farge traveled to Japan in 1886, and later to Ceylon and Samoa, he created quick landscape views, with jewel-like tones and piquant contrasts, which maintained a faithfulness to the atmosphere and emotion of the moment.

A key transitional figure between the nineteenth and twentieth centuries was Maurice Prendergast, one of the ablest American watercolorists to investigate impressionist theories in his work. He was born in Newfoundland in 1859 and raised and educated in Boston. His graphic skills were soon put to use when he became an apprentice to a postcard producer, but he yearned for greater exposure to new trends in painting. In the early 1890s he went to Paris, where he studied at the Académie Julien and soon came into contact with the style of the Nabis, a group of painters influenced by Gauguin's expressive use of color, particularly Bonnard, Vuillard, Signac and Denis. He also assimilated Whistler's impressionistic techniques, while his flat, planar descriptions of form can be attributed to the influence of Cézanne.

Over the course of the next two decades, Prendergast made six trips to cities in England, France and Italy. On his third journey he stayed in Venice for 18 months, sponsored by a wealthy American patron, Sarah Choate Sears, and was profoundly inspired by the waterways, bustling public plazas and rich architectural legacy of the city. In his sketches and paintings of Venice, he used systematic dabs of color to portray the figures; these resemble a pointillist technique, yet are less rigidly applied. A critic for the *Boston Evening Transcript* showered praise on these 'sparkling and gay pictures of that aqueous capital in its most festive moods. Mr Prendergast was born to paint fêtes and he carries a whole Fourth of July in his colorbox.'

Prendergast's subject matter was light-hearted, and he focused on strollers and celebrants in mosaic-like, dappled hues. He often included a fragment of the architecture of an historic building as a backdrop for the pulse of modern life moving around it, and he varied the tones in doorways and arches to prevent these elements from becoming static. He loved to include pretty, white-frocked women and girls carrying parasols, playing with hoops, or feeding pigeons in the squares. When Prendergast returned to America, he became a member of a progressive group of artists known as The Eight, which also included the urban realists Robert Henri, George Luks and John Sloan. They gathered at the MacBeth Gallery in New York in 1908, to exhibit work and to marshall their opposition to the conservative, establishment doctrines promoted by the National Academy of Design. Prendergast was also one of the central organizers of the 1913 Armory Show in New York, a very influential exhibition that was largely responsible for introducing modern art from Europe and beyond to America's shores.

Albert E Gallatin, whose *American Watercolorists*, published 1922, was the first authoritative text on the subject in America,

remarked that 'Childe Hassam is beyond any doubt the greatest exponent of Impressionism in America.' Born into a cultivated family in Dorchester, Massachusetts, in 1959, Hassam, like Prendergast, developed his mature watercolor style in the course of a three-year stay in Paris (1883-85), during which he became a devotee of the flickering strokes and brilliant palette of Monet. Although he received a thorough academic training at the Académie Julien, it was the glancing brushstrokes and vibrating surfaces of Impressionism that engrossed his attention. While in France, Hassam painted several peaceful, idyllic scenes of Chatou, a haven for artists on the Seine not far from La Grenouillère, where Monet and Renoir painted a famous series of boating parties.

Hassam's best known watercolors were produced in America during his summer visits in the 1890s to Appledore, on the Isle of Shoals off the coast of New Hampshire. Here his close friend, the poet Celia Thaxter, held convivial salons that drew talented artists and writers. Hassam began a delightful series of renderings of her garden which expressed a sympathetic connection with the prodigious floral studies of Monet. He crowded the paper with blossoms, offering no horizon line, just slashing strokes of brilliant primary hues in red, blue and yellow. Their slanted contours suggested the island breezes, and Hassam left plentiful areas of white to denote brilliant sunshine reflecting from the ocean.

Hassam was also inspired by the tonal, poetic effects of Whistler's watercolors, evident in Hassam's *Nocturne: Railway Crossing, Chicago* painted in 1893 for the World's Columbian Exposition in Chicago. The sheet is covered with dark blue washes depicting slick, rain-soaked streets, while thick dabs of yellow paint, applied straight from the tube, glow beyond the hansom cab to indicate streetcar lights and lampposts. A mood of evening mystery abounds in this small, fluid sketch.

Free from the commercial demands of magazine illustration, the work of Winslow Homer underwent a dramatic transformation during his two-year stay in Cullercoats, England. His compositions and brushwork displayed a new boldness that became the hallmark of his mature style and his subjects assumed a new heroic aspect. His watercolors ennobled the struggles of the Northumbrian fisherfolk against the turbulent waters of the North Sea. Homer would set out in a small dory in thunderous storms to observe the violent aspects of nature at the height of their force. The women he admired from a distance carrying creels of fish, mending nets and braving the gales were depicted with solid, almost sculptural limbs and pale white skin that recall classical Greek figures. His palette employed sober colors to reflect these more profound themes, as well as the somber hues

BELOW: Winslow Homer at his easel with *The Gulf Stream* in his painting room at Prout's Neck, Maine, silver print of unknown date

RIGHT: *The Etcher*, self-portrait by Frederick Childe Hassam, etching and drypoint, 7 x 4^{15}⁄$_{16}$ inches (National Portrait Gallery, Smithsonian Institution, Washington, D.C.)

ment of forms reveal Homer's interest in Japanese prints.

Homer's tropical views required a new, brighter range of colors to represent the strong contrasts between white buildings and boats, the sparkling, turquoise waters and the brilliant sunshine that radiated through the islands. He laid down several washes of startling intensity and skilful counterpoints of color in his compositions, which were simplified to a few key elements. The images had a deft, graphite underpinning and Homer rarely made changes, executing his brushstrokes with bravado, and only occasionally scraping away passages of white to evoke reflections of light.

Homer's watercolors were sought after during his lifetime. A show of his Adirondack watercolors at the Reichard Gallery in New York in 1890 sold out almost immediately, reflecting strong demand for his works, which he later marketed through Knoedler's in New York and Doll and Richards in Boston. After his death in 1910, his reputation scared. The Metropolitan Museum bought 12 watercolors that year; the Brooklyn Museum acquired 12 in 1911; and the Worcester Museum purchased 14 between 1908 and 1917. Their prices ranged from $540 to $2200, a considerable sum for watercolors at that time. A group of 49 Homer watercolors were displayed at the Carnegie Institute in Pittsburgh in 1923, and extolled by a reviewer. They possessed:

A freshness of a world far removed from that of our eighteenth-century academic beginnings. At the core of his work is a fund of that personality which in American art is the proud substitute for convention'.

As a *New York Tribune* critic had remarked in 1898:

Winslow Homer stands alone . . . He broke new ground, painted familiar subjects as no one had ever painted them before so that he seems to move in a world of his own.

John Singer Sargent's confirmed place among America's great watercolorists is a singular phenomenon, for he was neither born nor educated in the United States, and only lived there during the brief periods necessary to complete public mural projects and private portraiture commissions. Yet Sargent declined to forfeit his citizenship when offered the honor of a British knighthood and he ensured, through discussions with family members and his dealers, that his best watercolors would be sold in groups to prominent patrons and museum collections in America.

Sargent's parents were natives of Philadelphia, members of a well-educated and well-to-do class that often traveled to Europe in the late nineteenth century to acquire culture and status. As a child, Sargent was included on his mother's restless tours of galleries, museums and palaces. He later continued his education at the Ecole des Beaux Arts in Paris, and in the studio of Carolus Duran, a commercial portraitist devoted to the techniques of Velásquez. Sargent's career divides readily into two areas of achievement: his early acclaim and financial success as an incomparable society portraitist in Paris and London from 1870 to 1900; and his later mastery of the water-

of storm-darkened skies, ocean expanses, sturdy fishing boats and the sailors that worked them.

When Homer returned to America, he settled permanently in a studio at his family's compound at Prout's Neck, near Portland, Maine and continued to explore man's confrontations with nature, and his experiences in the wilderness. Most of the work that secured Homer's reputation was created after his 50th birthday, and consists principally of watercolors he produced on fishing expeditions to the north woods of the Adirondacks and Canada, and to the semi-tropical islands of Nassau in the Bahamas, Cuba, Bermuda and the Florida coast. He completed almost 700 watercolors in his lifetime and his awareness of his extraordinary gifts is underscored by his remark: 'You will see, in the future I will live by my watercolors.'

Winslow Homer and his brother Charles were members of the North Woods Club in Ausable, New York, and they devoted many of their visits to hunting and angling in the surrounding woods and lakes, usually in the company of Adirondack guides. Homer frequently depicted these people close-up in deep forest, celebrating man's ability to survive in remote and untrammeled territories. In his watercolor *Mink Pond*, Homer opted for a close-up perspective of the flora and fauna of a local site. Using iridescent tones, he highlighted a horizontal arrangement of a waterlily, a sunfish, a pair of butterflies and a frog, rendering them with unusual delicacy. The mood of immediacy and mystery, the deep color and the careful arrange-

color medium, creating virtuoso sketches of exotic and pictur-esque locales in Morocco, Tangiers, Venice and the Alps during the period from 1900 to his death. These latter paintings exhibit a spontaneity, lucidity and freshness that is testimony to the artist's pleasure in the vistas he described, far from the stultifying snobbery and limited creative opportunities he had endured among his elite portraiture clientele.

Sargent's expertise in character studies exhibited new vigor in quick renderings such as *Bedouins* (1905). The Arabs' dark-eyed faces possess a wary mystery, their white robes provide classical lines of drapery for Sargent to convey in layered blue washes of dazzling intensity. Sargent described the watercolor medium as 'making the best of an emergency,' and this intimate glimpse of foreign life has the immediacy of a candid photo-graph snapped close up. Sargent's draftsmanship was rarely better evidenced than in his seductive architectural images of palazzos and bridges along the sunlit waterways of Venice. Like Winslow Homer, he outfitted a gondola with his watercolor palettes and sketchbooks, drifting along the canals to discover original perspectives of such famous Venetian landmarks as the Rialto Bridge.

In a lively watercolor still-life, *Gourds*, Sargent adapted flickering, impressionistic brushwork to an all-over theme of lush vegetation and sensual fruit. Liquid, improvisational strokes of purple, red and turquoise seem almost messily applied as Sargent abandons his technical dexterity in favor of a mood of dappled light.

Sargent's first major show was in 1903 at the Carfax Gallery in London, and in 1904 he joined the Royal Society of Painters in Water-Colours. He was careful about the destination of his watercolors and often arranged to have them sold in groups. One such purchase by the Brooklyn Museum in 1909 netted him $20,000 for 86 works; part of the cost was raised by public subscription, an indication of the esteem Sargent's skills com-manded. His watercolors were often exhibited alongside Win-slow Homer's and, although their treatment of related subjects was often surprisingly similar, critics and reviewers preferred to contrast the two painters, establishing Homer's virility, love of nature and blunt directness in opposition to Sargent's re-finement, tact, elegance and exquisite hues.

Edward Hopper was born in 1882 and his deliberate, pains-takingly-wrought watercolors belong to the realistic conti-nuum that began with Thomas Eakins and was strengthened by Winslow Homer and John Singer Sargent. Hopper's dedication to pictorial accuracy is summed up in his statement:

My aim has always been the most exact transcription possible of my most in-timate impressions of nature.

Hopper was born in Nyack, on the Hudson River, just north of New York City. He studied illustration at Chase's New York School of Art, where he was taught by the legendary theorist, Robert Henri. Hopper made three trips to Europe between 1906 and 1910, staying mainly in Paris and its environs. On his return, he rented an apartment in New York, began a career in

commercial art, and spent his summers in Gloucester, Mas-sachusetts. The subjects of his watercolor studies during the 1920s were both urban and pastoral: clapboard houses and sun-lit streets in Gloucester, and desolate back alleys and railroad cars and crossings not far from his Manhattan flat. Hopper did not paint wet into wet, and his style was rarely fluid or sponta-neous. He shunned a pleasurable sense of the medium in favor of a cerebral detachment and objectivity that is so marked that his forms take on an element of the surreal.

Hopper worked directly from the subject and laid down care-ful layers of wash over a quick pencil sketch, developing a stark solidity to his shapes. What details were included were added with the tip of the brush. He painted his landscapes in the early morning or late evening, when no human presence was likely to intrude on the scene. The sharp shadows and isolated aspect of these views contributes to a powerful sense of solitude and alienation that symbolizes the loneliness of the post-war era. Hopper's *Mansard Roof* (1923) exhibits a looser handling of the medium than his later watercolors, with rare impressionistic flourishes in the brushstrokes to describe the trees and shadows. Nevertheless, the dominant character of the building, the cool northern light that pervades the palette, and the setting devoid of human figures are all characteristic of Hopper's style. This picture was displayed at the Brooklyn Museum's second water-color biennial and was purchased for the museum's collection. The artist's first sale in ten years, this encouraged Hopper to continue his intellectual experiments with the medium.

The standard-bearer for Modernist watercolors in America was John Marin, whose techniques embraced the brilliant hues of the Fauves and the daring compositional innovations of Cubists. Unlike Homer, Sargent and Hopper, John Marin was a watercolorist first and foremost, and during his prolific career created more than 3000 works in the medium.

Born in Rutherford, New Jersey, in 1870, Marin's primary professional training was in architecture, a subject he later adapted to a variety of urban schemes. He opened his own office in Union Hill, New Jersey, but it failed. Marin then began his artistic education at the Pennsylvania Academy of Fine Arts in 1899, before traveling to Europe for five years from 1905 to 1910, where he was profoundly influenced by the pastels and etchings of Whistler. Marin also displayed his watercolors at the 1907 Salon des Indépendants alongside Cézanne, Signac and Robert Delaunay.

In Paris, Marin became close friends with the photographer Edward Steichen, who later introduced him to Alfred Stieglitz in New York. Stieglitz was drawn to the watercolor medium because it favored intuitive, poetic approaches rather than cool, analytical description. He championed Marin's work at his Gallery 291 and featured it in one-man shows almost every

season. Marin's paintings were also exhibited in the Armory Show of 1913, the Forum Exhibition of Modern American Painters in 1916, and the Brooklyn Museum Survey of Contemporary Watercolors in 1921. His European sketches, such as *Clouds and Mountains at Kufstein*, employ colors with a muted, Whistlerian softness. The tiny village of Kufstein in the Austrian Tyrol is reduced to a pattern of pointillist dots, while billowing clouds blend with massive mountains in broad sweeps of lavender and blue washes above.

When Marin returned to New York he settled in Cliffside, New Jersey, and made summer pilgrimages to the Berkshires, the Adirondacks, New Mexico and Cape Split, Maine, where he made daringly chaotic interpretations of the coastline. His New York scenes emphasize the modern architectural wonders of skyscrapers, bursting with Futurist energy and staccato strokes. Marin disregarded the merely pretty for sites with impact, which he described with jagged lines and disjointed grids that at times appear almost crude. In his paintings of lower Manhattan, the bold, black outlines of railway girders and mechanical structures became his personal calligraphy. The confusion of forms suggest the aftermath of an explosion, and their dynamism entranced him:

You cannot create a work of art unless the things you behold respond to something within you. Therefore, if these buildings move me, they too must have life. Thus, the whole city is alive; buildings, people, all are alive; and the more they move me, the more I feel them to be alive.

LEFT: *Self-Portrait* by John Singer Sargent, 1892, oil on canvas, 21 × 17 inches (National Academy of Design, New York)

BELOW: *Study for 'A Sunday on La Grande Jatte'* by Georges Seurat, 1884, oil on canvas, 27¾ × 41 inches (The Metropolitan Museum of Art, New York, NY, bequest of Sam A. Lewisohn, 1951, 51.112.6)

Marin's studies of the Maine coastline were evocative rather than descriptive, ignoring specific topographical detail to suggest instead the mysterious force of nature. He used brilliant choppy strokes of color to convey the turbulent sea, and fleeting patches of brown and red pigments to depict vague land masses. Marin was not interested in sophisticated technique and applied tints with his fingers, with matchsticks, and even with the tips of syringes to achieve his desired effects. Marin continued productive until his death in 1953, aged 83, and received significant recognition during his lifetime. The Museum of Modern Art featured a major retrospective of his work in 1936 and *Look* magazine selected him as America's foremost artist in 1948. In addition, he represented the United States in the 25th Venice Biennale in 1950.

Another member of the avant-garde circle of artists promoted by Alfred Stieglitz was Charles Demuth. A specialist in watercolors, Demuth was born in Lancaster, Pennsylvania, in 1883 and, like Marin, attended the Pennsylvania Academy of Fine Arts, where he saw several examples of the older artist's work at the school's annual exhibitions. In his early landscapes Demuth paid homage to Marin's Tyrolean techniques, but despite the frequent comparisons critics drew between the two artists, Demuth was far more restrained and delicate in his presentation of forms. As Demuth commented:

John Marin and I drew our inspiration from the same sources. He brought his up in buckets and spilled much along the way. I dipped mine out with a teaspoon but I never spilled a drop.

Demuth made several trips to Paris prior to World War II, where he became friendly with Leo and Gertrude Stein and was exposed to Cubism. He returned to the bohemian art colony of Provincetown, Massachusetts, and developed close friendships with the American Cubist painter Stuart Davis and Marcel Duchamp, founder of the Dada movement. He often visited New York, where he was introduced to jazz and the Harlem nightclubs. His watercolors of circus figures, vaudeville acts and habitués of smoky *boites* have sinuous contours and blushes of tone that project an aura of romantic decadence. Their slightly shocking, vaguely immoral mood recalls the work of Toulouse-Lautrec. The frantic movement of his characters, whose forms seem to meld with their surroundings through blotting and planar manipulation, is a hallmark of the Futurists. Demuth also illustrated several novels, including Henry James' *The Turn of the Screw*, Emile Zola's *Nana*, and Frank Wedekind's *Pandora's Box*.

Demuth had been lame since childhood, and was plagued by ill-health throughout his life. The watercolor medium was far more portable and less strenuous, and he preferred its manageability, claiming, 'I'd much rather do watercolor. Oil paints are so messy.' When Demuth was diagnosed diabetic in the early 1920s, he returned to his family's homestead in Lancaster, where he carefully tended his mother's garden and executed a succession of exquisite still-lifes of flowers and vegetables. His simplified presentation of irises, poppies, gladioli and daisies,

which seem to float like faceted gems on the white page, owe a debt to the flattened space and angular forms of Cézanne. Demuth had seen a major show of Cézanne watercolors at the Montross Gallery in New York in 1916, and he interpreted Cézanne's geometries with mastery and grace, juxtaposing curves and intersecting diagonals and using sensitive, modulated color washes to create diaphanous forms. Like Cézanne, he left ample bare space on the sheet, and the mottled effects of color made his still-life objects advance and recede, creating a moving, breathing pictorial surface.

Although Demuth's forms possess a poetic quality, their technical control and clearly defined edges are evidence of Demuth's involvement with a movement known as Precisionism. The impetus for Precisionism had several sources: the clean, persistent geometries of the Russian Constructivists, the close-up, crystalline images of still-life objects produced by the photographers in the Stieglitz circle, and America's fascination with the machine-made perfection of the industrial age, whose technological improvements and architectural wonders burgeoned during the 1920s and 1930s.

BELOW: John Marin, Taos, New Mexico, photograph by Paul Strand, 1930, gelatin silver, 4¾ x 3⅝ inches (Collection of the J. Paul Getty Museum, Malibu, California)

RIGHT: *The Purple Pup* by Charles Demuth, c.1918, watercolor over graphite on paper, 8⅙ × 10⅞ inches (Courtesy of Museum of Fine Arts, Boston, MA Charles Henry Hayden Fund, 62.324)

Charles Sheeler's background and personal philosophies were closely aligned with those of Demuth. He was born in Philadelphia in 1883, attended the Pennsylvania Academy of Fine Arts, and toured Europe, before settling in Bucks County, Pennsylvania. He was a professional photographer and his watercolors show a predilection for hard edges, purity of line and clear hue. They focused on man-made landscapes such as *River Rouge Industrial Plant* (1928). The functional elements of buildings, towers and bridgework formed an interwoven patterning of verticals and horizontals, allowing sharp demarcations of light and dark masses, another legacy of modern photography. Sheeler's Precisionist works were still connected to actual settings and organic shapes, for he was not compelled to abandon realism, arguing that 'a picture could have incorporated into it the structural design implied in abstraction and be presented in a wholly realistic manner.'

Two artists who were friends and contemporaries of Demuth and Sheeler, and who made the leap into visions of pure abstraction, were Georgia O'Keeffe and Stuart Davis. O'Keeffe was raised in Sun Prairie, Wisconsin in the 1890s, attended the Art Institute of Chicago and later took classes at the Art Students' League in New York. While teaching in remote, rural elementary schools in Virginia and Texas, O'Keeffe came under the influence of Arthur Wesley Dow, a Modernist who encouraged her to reduce her paintings to basic compositional elements of line and color. O'Keeffe only painted watercolors early in her career, but she produced these with typical, single-minded absorption, sitting on the floor with the paper placed on the ground, and working with a wet-into-wet technique to mine the medium's fluid, accidental properties. Her *Blue* series of 1916 can be likened to textile designs, with an abbreviated graphic statement providing a subtext for provocative patterns of subtly changing hues rendered on tissue paper. Most of her watercolors, however, lack any pencil underpinning and though based on natural phenomena, such as *Pink and Green Mountains* (1917), they evolved into an ethereal, expressive and amorphous mode far beyond the realm of description.

O'Keeffe was Stieglitz's protegée and married him in 1924, although he displayed some of her watercolors as early as 1917. The paintings for which she is best known, however, are large-scale floral studies and images of animal skulls in oil, which are strictly observed in a manner more allied with Precisionism than with the free-flowing impulses of her watercolors.

Stuart Davis, like Charles Sheeler, was a Philadelphian, and he was born into a progressive, artistic family; his mother was a sculptor and his father was an art director for a publishing firm. He studied with Robert Henri in New York and began his career as an illustrator for *Harper's Weekly* and the radical journal, *The Masses*. He soon began to evolve his own version of the Synthetic Cubism developed by Picasso and Juan Gris, with its schematized scenes and unusual spatial relationships. In watercolors such as *Town Square*, Davis used flat patterns, oddly-angled buildings and high-contrast colors to underscore the energy of urban life. He drew his imagery from contemporary America, incorporating jazz music, highway culture, advertising signs, neon lights and ubiquitous arrows into a collage of dynamic forms. As a member of the Works Progress Adminis-

tration's federal art project, he prepared several planning studies in watercolor for large-scale murals. His watercolor and gouache sketch for *Swing Landscape Mural* offers a cacophony of color and form, abstractly devised and compressed into a busy jumble of lively planar forms suggesting building cranes, skyscrapers, telephone poles and syncopated billboard graphics.

A singular watercolorist whose landscapes, fraught with psychological import, delve into the shadowy regions of Surrealism, was the Ashtabula, Ohio native, Charles Burchfield. Burchfield's precocious talents earned him a scholarship to the National Academy of Design in 1916, following his graduation from the Cleveland School of Art. Lacking family means or sufficient sales of his work to support himself in New York, how-

ever, he subsequently returned to Ohio and worked first as an accountant, and later as a textile designer at the Birge Wallpaper Company in Buffalo, New York. What paintings he did sell were offered through the Sunrise Town Bookshop, a bookstore in Manhattan.

Burchfield's work possesses rhythmic patterns and a kind of visualized sound that enliven his surfaces in a manner often compared with Disney cartoon animation. He used distortions of form to amplify mood, and his spiky flowers and plants seem electrified and buzzing with life. There was no dead or empty space in his paintings; every stroke was filled with emotional content. His large-scale watercolors, with their dense mixture of transparent and opaque pigments, often appear to be oils, and he frequently reworked his images to achieve surprisingly solid forms, again reminiscent of oil.

The small-town world Burchfield describes in *February Thaw* is desolate to the point of the macabre; his empty buildings have anthropomorphic features, so that doors and windows seem like shifty eyes and gaping mouths. His plentiful use of deep black calligraphy, contrasted with pulsating yellow sunlight, added an extraordinary tension to his vistas. Strange halos around the moon and menacing clouds lent a nightmarish quality to many scenes. Burchfield's work gradually found a receptive audience through the efforts of the New York dealer Frank Rehn. His increasing popularity was reflected by the one-man exhibition the Museum of Modern Art gave him in 1930, and later in his life the National Academy of Design recognized his unusual talents with full membership in 1954.

Andrew Wyeth, another watercolor master, was born in 1917. His absorption with rural America, and fidelity to the stoically independent farm characters whose lives were tied to this landscape, set him apart from the experiments in abstraction and conceptual themes that characterized the work of many of his contemporaries. Wyeth is among the best known and most popular of American living artists and he has devoted his finely tuned draftsmanship to preserving the heritage of America's past, gleaning his subjects from the pastoral, agricultural world that surrounds him in Chadd's Ford, Pennsylvania and coastal Maine.

Wyeth was a fragile child, whose early artistic skills were honed while drawing in the studio alongside his famous father, N C Wyeth, one of the ablest illustrators of magazines, novels and commercial advertisements America has produced. Andrew's talents were apparent by his teens and at age 20 were publicly acknowledged in a one-man show held at the well-regarded MacBeth Gallery in New York. His early works, such as *The Coot Hunter* (1941), displayed a bravura and a fluid, confident brushwork far looser than his later paintings, for which he is best known. Following the death of his father and son in 1945, Andrew Wyeth tightened his style until it revealed almost microscopic details of ordinary, commonplace objects. His palette became limited to a range of earthy browns, ochers and grays, which enhanced a motif of weathering and a sense of time's erosion in his landscapes. He employed a dry brush technique in which almost all pigment was squeezed from the tip of the brush, and was then applied with infinite care to delineate facial wrinkles, plaster cracks in corroding stone houses, flaking paint on wooden boards, and selected blades of grass in the broad hayfields near his home.

Wyeth made extensive studies of the steadfast German im-

LEFT: Georgia O'Keeffe with Alfred Stieglitz, whom she married in 1924.

RIGHT: Charles Burchfield in his studio, c.1950, photographed by Herbert Appleton.

migrants who inhabited the Brandywine area of Pennsylvania, in particular the Kuerner family. He also painted the Olson family near Port Clyde in Maine. Their lives are depicted with a spareness to the point of impoverishment, and they are often shown individually, to imply both self-reliance and a kind of melancholy solitude. There is very little gesture or activity in Wyeth's portraits, which contributes to an aura of timelessness far removed from the restless haste of modern America and city dwellers. In the painting *Memorial Day* of 1946, Wyeth chose the site of a decrepit old building in Chadd's Ford known as Mother Archie's Church, where a black women's congregation met. Following a memorial service on June 4, 1946, for black soldiers who died during World War II, Wyeth espied a lone black man sitting in a pew and created a somber image with no visual distractions other than a large, fading American flag hung behind him. The otherwise bare walls and the emptiness of the room lend a sense of expectancy which is notable in many of Wyeth's watercolors and is created by what he has omitted. A similar effect is conveyed in *Karl's Room*, an interior devoid of any human presence except for a hunting rifle hanging from a dark wooden beam in the ceiling. Such objects are used to suggest the lingering presence of figures in the rooms, houses and even distant horizons the artist has painted. Andrew Wyeth has earned a unique place among twentieth-century watercolorists, and his roots are firmly planted in the incisive realism that is the legacy of Thomas Eakins and Winslow Homer.

A landmark exhibition at the Museum of Modern Art entitled 'Fantastic Art, Dada and Surrealism,' which was held during the winter of 1936 and 1937, set the tone for the avant-garde developments of the post-war era and the decades that followed. A search for universal symbols, rather than specific representations of settings and objects, and a pronounced interest in plumbing the subconscious mind, led to extraordinary changes in the treatment of watercolor surfaces and linear techniques. Emotional expression took the form of dream-like images with distorted shapes, highly animated brushstrokes, and a kind of abbreviated, dynamic calligraphy associated with primitive art.

Mark Rothko, born in 1903, and Jackson Pollock, born in 1912, were two of the more daring experimenters in the realm of automatism, a type of gestural transferral of psychic pictures on to the watercolor page. Rothko's early works were often large in scale, ranging up to three by four foot in size, and had a hazy, pulsating quality. Loose, liquid masses, suggesting dismembered body parts, were connected with lyrical, spidery lines. His floating, atmospheric layers of transparent wash suggest an underwater environment, while the unpredictable collisions of various elements seem at times to reflect the moral uncertainties of contemporary political and cultural events.

Jackson Pollock, a native of Cody, Wyoming, gravitated to New York, where he studied with the regionalist Thomas Hart Benton at the Art Students' League during the early 1940s. Pollock found that Benton's strong personality provoked him to positive opposition, to push in his own directions and to defy the limits of the rules of art. For his part, Benton felt that Pollock's wildly energetic paintings, which appeared to be achieved spontaneously 'correspond to the actual mechanics of human vision, which is also without closed peripheries.'

Several of Pollock's early drawings and watercolors were created at the suggestion of his psychiatrist, as a therapeutic device to resolve internal conflicts. Several of these paintings display a jagged, frenzied line punctuated with deep opaque color, and a brutal, sometimes violent, sense of struggle emerges from their tempestuous contours. The smaller scale of the watercolor medium allowed Pollock to investigate formal concepts of design that later evolved into his highly original 'action' paintings in oil on canvas.

The lyrical, sunlit statements of Sam Francis, born in 1923, are as nonrepresentational as those by Rothko and Pollock, yet the paint is more controlled and directed in its passage across the watercolor sheet. Francis allows blots and bars of bright color both to divide the picture surface and to bleed and pool together in elegant arrangements. The white areas are left sparkling fresh, significant pauses that hint at sunlight in landscapes, and the overall image has the effervescence of Chinese scrolls. A spattering of delicate, calligraphic scribbles are overlaid by flicking a loaded brush on to the page. The pleasures of the medium itself, free from restrictions of narrative content, are paramount in Francis' works and they charm with a childlike naiveté.

Claes Oldenburg, though primarily a sculptor, has used watercolor as a preparatory phase in planning his preposterous, colossal sculptures, which transform ordinary objects into art monuments. Imagination and humor are the keynotes of his style and his watercolors seem a hybrid cross between architectural renderings and cartoon fantasies. Oldenburg was born in Stockholm, Sweden, in 1939 and raised in the United States, where he joined the Pop Art movement of the 1960s, devising jokey sculptures of gigantic hamburgers, huge melting tubes of lipstick, outrageously large erasers, and even a monstrous vacuum cleaner for a public plaza at Battery Park in New York. Oldenburg's whimsical watercolor of a vast clothes pin, an entry to the Chicago Tribune's competition for a city monument, illustrates the playful, conceptual aspects of Pop Art, which raised the commonplace and commercial facets of American culture to the hallowed sphere of fine art.

Chuck Close, on the other hand, is among the most cerebral of modern artists, who has dedicated his sublime powers of scrutiny to examining idiosyncrasies of the human face, and focusing steadfastly on the process whereby its features coalesce into a unified whole. In contrast to earlier portrait painters such as John Singer Sargent, Close makes no attempt to render judgment, treating all facial elements equally, and without endeavoring to highlight good features or hide flaws. He begins with a photographic enlargement, yet his work goes beyond the glossy allure of photorealism to uncover the method by which colored marks, precisely placed in grids in a manner akin to pointillism, satisfy the informational requirements of a particular sitter's presence. His technical expertise and notably arbitrary approach to a subject, charged with ideals of beauty and ugliness, make the paintings of Chuck Close a kind of bridge between the careful realism of Thomas Eakins and the cool objectivity of the medium of television.

Over the course of a century and a half, watercolor has responded to the needs of American artists. Its uniquely translucent light effects, and its easy preparation and application have made it wonderfully adaptable to the mobile population of a vast geographical expanse. It has prevailed through a panoply of art movements, from the Hudson River School to Impressionism, Social Realism, Cubism, Surrealism, Abstract Expressionism, Pop Art and Conceptualism, while maintaining its integrity as a graphic art form especially suited to linear experimentation and nuances of color.

America's watercolor painters have reveled in quick, topographical sketches of their country's beauty and incisive, carefully rendered portraits of its athletes and citizens. These paintings are a record of changing developments in the fine arts and in the social fabric of American culture. More contemporary inquiries into psychological domains and technological processes express a great range of freedom and spontaneity, attributes of both the watercolor medium and the American psyche which promise both a compelling future.

ABOVE LEFT: *The Corner* by Andrew Wyeth, 1953, dry brush and watercolor on paper, 13½ × 21½ inches (Delaware Art Museum, Wilmington, DE, gift of Mr and Mrs W. E. Phelps)

below: *Late Submission to the Chicago Tribune Architectural Competition of 1922: Clothespin (Version Two)*, 1967, pencil, crayon and watercolor on paper, 22 × 23¼ inches (Des Moines Art Center Permanent Collection, IA, partial purchase with funds from Gardner Cowles and gift of Charles Cowles, 1972.11)

WATERCOLOR'S BEGINNINGS

The breadth of America's commercial and cultural ties with Great Britain during the nineteenth century fostered an exchange of artistic techniques and theories between the two countries. Several of America's early watercolorists were emigrants from England, who arrived thoroughly versed in lithography, aquatints and watercolor.

William Guy Wall was an Irish immigrant who arrived in New York in 1818; his views of New York and its surrounding sites are peaceful summer vistas with a strong horizontal emphasis. His palette favored delicate blue, green and brown washes, and figures and foliage are laid in with stippling, to convey detail. The trees and land masses are schematized, and though Wall includes schooners on the waterways to emphasize America's maritime power, they are becalmed. The overall impression is rather static, favoring topographical detail over feeling.

John William Hill is best remembered for his close-up studies of plants and birds, painted in the precise, reportorial style expounded by the Pre-Raphaelite theorist John Ruskin. Hill's *Study of Fruit* (1877) has a careful, almost pedantic, graphite underpinning, over which layers of delicate washes are laid and miniaturist detail is added with tiny brushes. No part of the white paper is untouched, and highlights such as the opaque white pigment on the apple appear to be reflected sunlight.

George Inness was born in 1824 into a cultivated family in Newburgh, New York. After early studies at an engraving firm and in a French painter's studio, he made an auspicious debut at the National Academy of Design at the age of 20. A New York auctioneer sponsored Inness' first trip to Europe in 1851 and he returned on several occasions during his lifetime. Inness' style was far more informal and poetic than that of the Pre-Raphaelites and Hudson River School artists. In his *Castle in Mountains*, Inness chose a panoramic view not far from Titian's birthplace in Pieve de Cadore, Italy, employing loosely applied washes over generalized graphite forms of trees, hills and floating clouds. His style is closely attuned to that of the British painter, J M W Turner. In 1840 a British artist named Frederick Catherwood brought 500 of Turner's drawings and watercolors to the United States, introducing his romantic fantasies of sunwashed skies and dazzling horizons to the American public.

William Trost Richards applied the Ruskinian principles of dedication to nature and exactitude of description to the seacoast scenes he encountered on summer pilgrimages to Atlantic City and Newport, Rhode Island. His large painting *Near Paradise, Newport* is on a scale to compete with oils of the era. His use of opaque pigments and tiny brushes creates solid forms of the rock outcroppings and botanically detailed lichen and shore flowers he depicts. There is a sense of specificity of place borne of many hours of deliberate observation.

Thomas Moran perfected his watercolor skills as the staff artist on Ferdinand Hayden's expedition to the Yellowstone region of the American West. His *Cliffs of the Rio Virgin, South Utah* (1873), possesses the monumentality and sweep of horizontal space that are also keynotes of Turner's style. His layers of tinted wash evoke scale and nuance, and while some prominent aspects are defined, others coalesce into misty anonymity.

In contrast to Moran, Thomas Eakins directed his carefully scientific scrutiny to the human figure to create a series of probing and detached character studies. He was drawn to the figure of John Biglin, a professional oarsman he encountered while sculling on the Schuylkill River. He took particular care to stress Biglin's musculature and poise in his watercolor, so that the athlete evokes the solidity and strength of classical sculpture. In *Baseball Players Practicing*, Eakins placed the central figures' heads near the continuous horizontal line of the bleacher's railing in the background. It is late in the afternoon and the sun casts dramatic shadows on the players, who stand prepared as if anticipating an event beyond the borders of the picture.

RIGHT ABOVE
William Guy Wall
View Near Fishkill, n.d.
Watercolor on paper (mounted on cardboard)
Collection of the New-York Historical Society New York, NY (1903.14)

RIGHT BELOW
William Guy Wall
The Bay of New York Taken from Brooklyn Heights, 1820-25
Watercolor on white wove paper, 21⅜ × 32¾ inches
The Metropolitan Museum of Art, New York, NY, the Edward W. C.
Arnold Collection of New York Prints, Maps and Pictures,
bequest of Edward W. C. Arnold, 1954 (54. 90. 158)

John William Hill
Bird's Nest and Dogroses, 1867
Watercolor on paper, 18 × 24 inches
Collection of the New-York Historical Society, New York, NY (1947.519)

John William Hill
Landscape: View on Catskill Creek, 1867
Watercolor, gouache and graphite underdrawing on off-white
wove paper, 9¹¹⁄₁₆ × 15¹⁄₁₆ inches
The Metropolitan Museum of Art, New York, NY, gift of John
Henry Hill, 1882 (82.9.6)

John William Hill
Study of Fruit, 1877
Watercolor over graphite on paper, 6⅛ × 10⅝ inches
Courtesy of Museum of Fine Arts Boston, MA, M. and M. Karolik
Collection (55.753)

ABOVE
George Inness
Castle in Mountains, c.1873
Watercolor over graphite on paper, 8⅞ × 12 inches
Courtesy of Museum of Fine Arts, Boston, MA, M. and M. Karolik
Collection (60.1026)

RIGHT ABOVE
William Trost Richards
Beach with Sun Drawing Water, 1872
Watercolor, 6¾ × 13⅞ inches
Courtesy of Museum of Fine Arts, Boston, MA, M. and M. Karolik
Collection (60.1058)

RIGHT BELOW
William Trost Richards
Sundown at Centre Harbor, New Hampshire, 1874
Watercolor, gouache and graphite on green wove paper, 8⅞ × 13⅝ inches
The Metropolitan Museum of Art, New York, NY, gift of the
Reverend E. L. Magoon, D.D., 1880 (80.1.1)

William Trost Richards
Near Paradise, Newport, 1877
Watercolor over graphite on paper, 23 × 37 inches
Courtesy of Museum of Fine Arts, Boston, MA, gift of Mrs
Arthur Astor Carey (Res. 27.124)

ABOVE
Thomas Moran
Cliffs of the Rio Virgin South Utah, 1873
Watercolor, white gouache over graphite on light brown wove paper, 16 × 22 inches
Cooper-Hewitt Museum, Smithsonian Institution/Art Resource New York NY (1917-17-20)

LEFT
Thomas Moran
Chicago World's Fair, 1894
Watercolor over pencil on paper, 29 × 21½ inches, slightly irregular
The Brooklyn Museum, NY, bequest of Clara L. Obrig (31.194)

Thomas Eakins
John Biglen in a Single Scull, c.1873
Watercolor on paper, 17⅛ × 23 inches
The Metropolitan Museum of Art, New York, NY, Fletcher Fund,
1924 (24.108)

Thomas Eakins
Baseball Players Practicing, 1875
Watercolor on paper, 10⅞ × 12⅞ inches
Museum of Art, Rhode Island School of Design, Providence, RI, Jesse Metcalf
and Walter H. Kimball Funds

Thomas Eakins
Negro Boy Dancing, 1878
Watercolor on paper, 18⅛ × 22⅝ inches
The Metropolitan Museum of Art, New York, NY, Fletcher Fund,
1925 (25.97.1)

Thomas Eakins
Taking up the Net, 1881
Watercolor on off-white wove paper, 9½ × 14¹⁄₁₆ inches
The Metropolitan Museum of Art, New York, NY, Fletcher Fund,
1925 (25.97.3)

37

IMPRESSIONISM

During the late nineteenth century, technological improvements in transatlantic shipping made travel abroad an inviting proposition for America's leisure classes. The intellectual and artistic elite followed their wealthy patrons to Europe in a quest for polish and sophistication, as well as exposure to the treasures of its palaces and museums and the teachings of its well-regarded academies. James Abbott McNeill Whistler was a trailblazer among expatriate American artists and one of the first to embrace the tenets of Impressionism, which dramatically altered the palettes, compositions and personal approaches of many American watercolorists. Whistler lived in both Paris and London and traveled often to Rome, Venice and the Netherlands. Counted among his close friends were the artists Edgar Degas, Edouard Manet and Claude Monet.

Whistler's beach scenes and seascapes, such as *Nocturne: Grand Canal, Amsterdam* and *Sailboats in Blue Water*, were notable for their poetic inspiration and their immediacy. The artist fashioned quick sketches on site with little or no graphite underpinning, painting wet-into-wet with a bold directness and limited palette to express the delicate moods of nature. His gift for gesture is also revealed in a small portrait, *Milly Finch*, whose alluring pose readily captures the sense of luxury and the elegant appeal of European salon settings.

John La Farge was born of wealthy French emigré parents in 1835, and after graduating from college traveled to Europe, where he studied in the Paris studio of Thomas Couture, absorbing the technical mastery of the Barbizon painters. His intimate, notational watercolors were spontaneous and relaxed. In *Wild Roses in an Antique Chinese Bowl*, he expressed the translucency of blossoms by overlapping delicate layers of washes. La Farge was a devotee of Japanese art and described his working methods as 'veilings and sequences' gleaned from Oriental prints. He visited Japan in 1886 and Ceylon and Samoa in 1891, and captured *View in Ceylon, near Dambulla, Looking Down Over Rice-Fields* while visiting a cave-site filled with Buddhist sculpture. The image is misty and decorative,

highlighted by a jewel-like border of azure cliffs on the right and fragile native trees and shrubs. It is surprisingly panoramic for a sketch measuring only 13 by 17 inches.

Following an apprenticeship to a Boston postcard producer, Maurice Prendergast enrolled at the Académie Julien in Paris and later lived in Venice, sponsored by a wealthy American patron. In France, Prendergast's style was strongly influenced by members of the Nabis, including Bonnard, Signac and Vuillard. He began to employ systematic dabs of color in his watercolors, reminiscent of the pointillist technique. In *Piazza di San Marco*, Prendergast uses three large, bright, Italian banners to establish a sense of public scale and festivity. The flags crop the classical structure of the architecture on the right side of the picture, and their colors are picked up in the animated dots that signify tourists streaming through the square. In *Umbrellas in the Rain*, the artist creates a mosaic of brief patches of color, enhanced by reflections in puddles on the sidewalk. The pooling and bleeding of hues underscores the fluid presence of Venice's waterways in the background. Plentiful passages of white are noted in the dresses of the ladies and children, creating a feeling of light, openness and gaiety on an otherwise gloomy day. The flatness of his patterns, his imprecise figures and shapes, and his vivid palette reveal his strong impressionist tendencies.

Like Prendergast, Childe Hassam studied at the Académie Julien in Paris for several years, but he was most drawn to the work of the Impressionists, especially Claude Monet. Hassam's best known watercolors are a series of buoyant sketches fashioned in the 1890s and later, during his summer visits to Appledore on the Isle of Shoals in New Hampshire. There he was a member of a coterie of talented writers and artists who stayed at the home of the poet Celia Thaxter. In his images of her garden, he combined a bold color scheme of intense primary hues with slashing strokes and flickering calligraphy to capture the essence of sun-dappled foliage and ocean breezes. His gestural, linear patterns go beyond mere description and can be enjoyed independently of representational content.

RIGHT ABOVE
James McNeill Whistler
Grey and Silver: Pier, Southend, early 1880s
Watercolor on paper
Courtesy of the Freer Gallery of Art, Smithsonian Institution, Washington, D.C. (02.169)

RIGHT BELOW
James McNeill Whistler
Nocturne: Grand Canal, Amsterdam
Watercolor on paper, 8¹⁵⁄₁₆ × 11³⁄₁₆ inches
Courtesy of the Freer Gallery of Art, Smithsonian Institution, Washington, D.C. (02.161)

James McNeill Whistler
Millie Finch, early 1880s
Watercolor on paper, 11⁹⁄₁₀ x 9 inches
Courtesy of the Freer Gallery of Art, Smithsonian Institution,
Washington, D.C. (07.170)

James McNeill Whistler
Sailboats in Blue Water, n.d.
Watercolor on off-white paper, 8⅜ × 4⅞ inches
Courtesy of the Fogg Art Museum, Harvard University Art
Museums, Cambridge, MA, bequest of Grenville L. Winthrop
(1943.332)

231

LEFT
John La Farge
Wild Roses and Irises, 1887
Gouache and watercolor on white wove paper, 14½ × 10⁷⁄₁₆ inches
The Metropolitan Museum of Art, New York, NY, gift of
Priscilla A. B. Henderson, 1950, in memory of her grandfather,
Russell Sturgis, a founder of the Metropolitan Museum of Art
(50.113.3)

ABOVE
John La Farge
Seascape, c.1883
Watercolor on paper, 6¹¹⁄₁₆ × 4⅞ inches
Courtesy of Museum of Fine Arts, Boston, MA, gift of Miss Mary
C. Wheelwright (59.688)

ABOVE
John La Farge
Wild Roses in an Antique Chinese Bowl, 1880
Watercolor on paper, 10⅞ × 9⅟₁₆ inches
Courtesy of Museum of Fine Arts, Boston, MA, bequest of
Elizabeth Howard Bartol (27.96)

RIGHT
John La Farge
Mountain Gorge Near Dambulla, Ceylon
Watercolor on paper, 16¾ × 13½ inches
Courtesy of Museum of Fine Arts, Boston, MA, bequest of
William Sturgis Bigelow (26.784)

Maurice Prendergast
Handkerchief Point, 1896
Watercolor, 20 × 13¾ inches
Courtesy of Museum of fine Arts, Boston, MA, gift of Frances
W. Fabyan in memory of Edith Westcott Fabyan (31.906)

ABOVE
Maurice Prendergast
Umbrellas in the Rain, Venice, 1899
Watercolor over graphite on paper, 13¹⁵⁄₁₆ × 20⅞ inches
Courtesy of Museum of Fine Arts, Boston, MA, Hayden Collection Charles Henry
Hayden Fund (1959.57)

Maurice Prendergast
Court Yard, West End Library, Boston, 1901
Watercolor, graphite and charcoal on off-white wove paper, 14⅞ × 21½ inches
The Metropolitan Museum of Art, New York, NY, gift of estate
of Mrs Edward Robinson, 1952 (52.126.7)

Maurice Prendergast
Piazza di San Marco, c. 1898
Watercolor and graphite on white wove paper, 16¹¹⁄₁₆ × 15³⁄₈ inches
The Metropolitan Museum of Art, New York, NY, gift of estate
of Mrs Edward Robinson, 1952 (52.126.6)

49

ABOVE
Maurice Prendergast
Long Beach, 1920-23
Watercolor, pencil and black ink on paper, 15½ × 22½ inches
Courtesy of Museum of Fine Arts, Boston, MA, Hayden
Collection, Charles Henry Hayden Fund (50.652)

RIGHT
Frederick Childe Hassam
Isle of Shoals Garden or *Garden in its Glory*, 1892
Watercolor on paper, 19¹⁵⁄₁₆ × 13⅞ inches
National Museum of American Art, Smithsonian Institution,
Washington, D.C., gift of John Gellatly/ Art Resource,
New York, NY (1929.6.56)

50

LEFT
Frederick Childe Hassam
Nocturne, Railway Crossing, Chicago, 1893
Watercolor on paper, 16 × 11¾ inches
Courtesy of Museum of Fine Arts, Boston, MA, Hayden Collection, Charles Henry
Hayden Fund (62.986)

ABOVE
Frederick Childe Hassam
The Gorge, Appledore, 1912
Watercolor on paper, 13¾ × 19⅞ inches
The Brooklyn Museum, NY, Museum Collection Fund (24.103)

Frederick Childe Hassam
Sunday Morning, Appledore, 1912
Watercolor on paper, 13⁹⁄₁₆ × 19⁹⁄₁₆ inches
The Brooklyn Museum, NY, Museum Collection Fund (31.104)

Frederick Childe Hassam
Street in Portsmouth, 1916
Watercolor on off-white wove paper, 15⅛ × 22 inches
The Metropolitan Museum of Art, New York, NY, Rogers Fund, 1917 (17.31.2)

MASTER REALISTS

As his biographer, the art historian Lloyd Goodrich, proclaimed, 'The man who more than any other raised watercolor to the artistic level of oil was Winslow Homer.' It is alongside Homer that all other American watercolorists are judged, and his best paintings offer a kind of litmus test for determining freshness of color, integrity of line, and visual delight in the natural bounty of America's varied landscapes.

Homer's draftsmanship was honed as an apprentice lithographer at Bufford's in Boston. During a two-year sojourn in the tiny Northumberland fishing village of Cullercoats, England, Homer's style underwent a metamorphosis from his early sweetness and sentimentality, projecting a more serious and heroic aspect into the vigorous marine vistas that he favored, with their solitary figures pursuing a dangerous livelihood. In the painting *Afterglow*, there is evidence of Homer's inventive techniques of blotting, scraping and repainting to strengthen his original scheme. The vibrant contrast between the glowing orange sky and deep blue boats is a Homer trademark.

When Homer returned to America, he settled in a studio at his family compound at Prout's Neck in Maine. Most of his watercolors of the 1880s and 1890s were produced on fishing and hunting trips to the Adirondacks, Canada and Florida, and they are among his finest paintings. In *Deer Drinking* he focuses on a large, central subject described with plentiful layers of wash. Homer has chosen an unusual pose, with the shy, wild animal pictured close-up so that the viewer feels drawn into the scene.

John Singer Sargent's genius with the watercolor medium developed from very different sources from Winslow Homer's talent. Sargent was born in Florence, and educated at the Ecole des Beaux Arts in Paris and in the studio of Carolus Duran, a commercial portraitist. A superb draftsman, Sargent perfected his virtuoso brushwork as a society portraitist in Paris and London from 1870 to 1900, acquiring a marked ability to render textures, fabrics, patterns and light sources. Despite the significant following and financial success earned by his portraits, however, Sargent grew increasingly irritated with the petty criticisms of his clientele, and bored with their stultifying snobbery and indolent lifestyle. Free from monetary concerns, he set off for more exotic locales, such as Tangiers, Jerusalem, Venice, the Swiss Alps and Canadian Rockies. His watercolors of these sites express a pleasure in and abandonment to spontaneous effects of light and brush that is absent from his restrained and deliberate portraits. The extreme close-up perspective of schooners and their riggings in Sargent's watercolor *In A Levantine Port* allows for more gestural calligraphy and flickering, impressionistic brushwork than one might see in a Homer painting of a similar subject. Slashing strokes of turquoise, purple, yellow and brown intersect and meld with extraordinary fluidity. Areas of white on the paper are augmented with dashes of opaque white pigment for highlights.

After the bravura flourishes and brilliant light of Sargent's foreign landscapes, the watercolors of Edward Hopper appear restrained and cool to the point of melancholy. There is nothing romantic or facile in the urban landscapes and coastal lighthouses Hopper painted, yet his dedication to the realist vernacular and the strength of his austere compositions aligns him with Homer and Sargent. Hopper was at his best exploring architectural themes. In *Highland Light (North Truro)* the vertical shape of the lighthouse dominates a cold, barren landscape. Although a road leading to its cluster of outbuildings is included, there is little sense of welcome or of the traditional protection offered by a lighthouse dwelling. Unlike Sargent, Hopper was uninterested in decorative schemes and alluring colors, preferring a plain, objective palette and highly reductive structural elements. He often painted in the early morning or late evening, when no one would intrude on his scenes and the sun or moon cast sharp, almost menacing shadows.

Andrew Wyeth is one of the few later-twentieth-century watercolorists dedicated to painting America's pastoral farmlands and the independent characters who inhabit them, in a determined effort to preserve the rural heritage of America's past. Wyeth's choice of subjects is preoccupied with the ordinary and commonplace: weathered, abandoned buildings in wide-open fields; aging, impoverished farmhands and country people; interiors of old houses that seem fully inhabited by the presence of those personalities who once lived in them. In *Wood Stove* he depicts the telltale signs of hardship that Christina Olson, a polio victim, has endured through years of confinement. The window shade is cracked, the ceiling is peeling, the geraniums look almost crippled seeking light in a dark room. An overwhelming sense of loneliness also pervades the pale, empty chamber of *Up in the Studio*. The room is full of gray shadows, broken plaster, brown floorboards and little else. Echoes of former lives reverberate in Wyeth's settings. Few American artists have so successfully distilled a sense of timelessness and charged emotion within such a restrained pictorial framework.

Winslow Homer
Prout's Neck Breakers, 1883
Watercolor, 14¾ × 21⅛ inches
© 1994 The Art Institute of Chicago, IL, Mr and Mrs Martin A Ryerson
Collection (1933.1247), all rights reserved

Winslow Homer
Afterglow, 1883
Watercolor on paper, 14¼ × 21 inches
Courtesy of Museum of Fine Arts, Boston, MA, bequest
of William P. Blake in memory of his mother, Mary M.J. Dehon
Blake (47.1202)

Winslow Homer
The Mink Pond, 1891
Watercolor over graphite on heavy white woven paper, 14 × 21 inches
Courtesy of the Fogg Art Museum, Harvard University Art
Museums, Cambridge, MA, bequest of Grenville L. Winthrop
(1943.304)

Winslow Homer
Deer Drinking, 1892
Watercolor, 14⅟₁₆ × 20⅟₁₆ inches
Yale Univesity Art Gallery, New Haven, CT, the Robert W. Carle
fund (1976.36)

Winslow Homer
Taking on Wet Provisions, 1903
Watercolor and graphite on white wove paper, 14 × 21¾ inches
The Metropolitan Museum of Art, New York, NY,
Amelia B. Lazarus Fund, 1910 (10.288.11)

LEFT ABOVE
John Singer Sargent
Gourds, *c*.1905-08
Watercolor on paper, 14 × 20 inches
The Brooklyn Museum, NY, purchased by special subscription (09.882)

LEFT BELOW
John Singer Sargent
Muddy Alligators, 1917
Watercolor over graphite on medium, textured cream wove paper, 13½ × 20⅞ inches
Worcester Art Museum, Worcester, MA, Sustaining Membership Fund (1917.86)

ABOVE
John Singer Sargent
Bedouins, *c*.1905-06
Watercolor on paper, 18 × 12 inches
The Brooklyn Museum, NY, purchased by special subscription (09.814)

John Singer Sargent
In a Levantine Port, c.1905-06
Watercolor and pencil on paper, 12$\frac{1}{16}$ × 18$\frac{1}{8}$ inches
The Brooklyn Museum, NY, purchased by special subscription (09.825)

John Singer Sargent
Reading, 1911
Watercolor on paper, 20 × 14 inches
Courtesy of Museum of Fine Arts, Boston, MA, Hayden
Collection, purchased Charles Henry Hayden Fund (12.214)

John Singer Sargent
A Tent in the Rockies, c. 1916
Watercolor on paper, 15⅜-15½ × 20¹⁄₁₆ inches
Isabella Stewart Gardner Musuem, Boston, MA (P3W17)

John Singer Sargent
Under the Rialto Bridge, 1909
Watercolor over graphite on paper, 10⅞ × 19 inches
Courtesy of Museum of Fine Arts, Boston, MA, Hayden Collection, Charles Henry
Hayden Fund (12.203)

ABOVE
Edward Hopper
Deck of a Beam Trawler, 1923
Watercolor over graphite on paper, 11¹⁵⁄₁₆ × 18 inches
Courtesy of Museum of Fine Arts, Boston, MA, Bequest of John T. Spaulding
(48.715)

OVERLEAF
Edward Hopper
The Mansard Roof, 1923
Watercolor over pencil on paper, 14 × 20 inches
The Brooklyn Museum, NY, Museum Collection Fund (23.100)

PREVIOUS PAGES
Edward Hopper
Highland Light (North Truro), 1930
Watercolor over graphite on white paper, 16½ × 25½ inches
Courtesy of the Fogg Art Museum, Harvard University Art
Museums, Cambridge, MA (1930.462)

76

Andrew Newell Wyeth
The Wood Stove, n.d.
Watercolor (drybrush), 23 × 34 inches
William A. Farnsworth Library and Art Museum, Rockland, ME,
museum purchase (62.1266)

Andrew Newell Wyeth
Alvaro and Christina, n.d.
Watercolor on paper, 22 × 29 inches
William A. Farnsworth Library and Art Museum, Rockland ME,
museum purchase (69.1646)

Andrew Newell Wyeth
The Coot Hunter, 1941
Watercolor, 17 × 28¹¹⁄₁₆ inches
© 1994 The Art Institute of Chicago, IL, Olivia Schaler Swan Memorial
Fund (1943.757), all rights reserved

Andrew Newell Wyeth
Memorial Day, 1946
Watercolor over graphite on paper, 14 × 20 inches
Courtesy of Museum of Fine Arts, Boston, MA, Charles Henry
Hayden and Abraham Shuman Funds (46.1455)

Andrew Newell Wyeth
Up in the Studio, 1965
Drybrush on paper, 17 × 23⅞ inches
Jointly owned by The Metropolitan Museum of Art, New York, NY,
and Amanda K. Berls, 1966 (66.216)

MODERNISM ARRIVES

John Marin was a prolific watercolorist who stood at the forefront of Modernism in America. A key organizer of the 1913 Armory Show, which brought the startling work of the Fauve painters, Matisse and Derain, and the Cubists, Picasso and Gris to the United States, Marin assimilated the brilliant palette of the former and the fragmented surface formats of the latter into his dynamic watercolors of the Manhattan skyline and evocative images of coastal Maine. Marin's personal, urban vocabulary consisted of jagged black outlines to suggest city girders and railroad bridges. Bright passages of red, blue and yellow burst from within, as if the network of skyscrapers and transit lines were exploding with life. In *Red Sun, Brooklyn Bridge*, Marin was intent on capturing the dynamic pulse of contemporary life within a rapidly sketched framework of diagonal lines. His Maine paintings were more evocative than descriptive, abandoning landscape detail in favor of transitory delights in works such as his *Crotch Island, Maine Coast* (1919).

Charles Demuth employed techniques akin to Marin, yet expressed them with a far more restrained palette and a sensitivity to edges and intersecting shapes influenced primarily by Cézanne. His smoky, transparent watercolors of cafés and nightclubs are rendered in dreamlike, overlapping washes to convey both the kinetic synchronicity of the Futurists and the decadent romanticism associated with the posters of Toulouse-Lautrec. In his later years, Demuth suffered from diabetes and retired to his mother's farmhouse in Lancaster, Pennsylvania, where he produced exquisite still lifes of the flowers and vegetables he tended in her garden.

A similar network of lines overlaid with wash breaks up the horizon in Lyonel Feininger's image of *The River*. Feininger was born in New York in 1871 but later went to Germany, where he became a member of the Bauhaus school. His interest in reductive compositions produced stylized mechanical renderings with architectonic echoes that link him with the Precisionist movement in America. The leading practitioner of Precisionism was a Pennsylvania artist and photographer, Charles Sheeler, who concentrated his artistic efforts on functional objects and man-made landscapes, such as the factory scene in *River Rouge Industrial Plant*.

Georgia O'Keeffe was Alfred Stieglitz's favorite protégée. Though her best-known oils are close-up perspectives of flowers and animal skulls, her early watercolors were brave experiments in abstraction, extracting and simplifying the essence of particular events into bold line and fluid, primary color. Like O'Keeffe, Stuart Davis adapted real objects from an observed landscape into a syncopated formal design alive with symbols, color and sound.

Charles Burchfield's watercolors of small-town streets and rural vistas are so highly charged with emotion and allusions to sound they seem to buzz. Often compared to the animated cartoons of Walt Disney, Burchfield's paintings are imbued with a panoply of spiky plants, menacing clouds, haloed moons, vibrating sunbursts and Gothic buildings, whose windows leer and whose doors appear like gaping mouths. Burchfield lived first in Ashtabula, Ohio, and later in Buffalo, where he worked as a wallpaper designer far from the influences of the Manhattan art world. Yet his paintings are fraught with the macabre, psychological tension of the German Expressionists, and his freely applied, surging patterns of contrasting brushstrokes are modern examples of both wonder and angst.

RIGHT ABOVE
John Marin
River Effect, Paris, 1909
Watercolor on paper, 13 × 16 inches
Philadelphia Museum of Art, PA, A. E. Gallatin Collection (52.61.73)

RIGHT BELOW
John Marin
Red Sun, Brooklyn Bridge, c.1922
Watercolor with charcoal on white wove paper, 21³⁄₁₆ × 25¹⁵⁄₁₆ inches
© 1994 The Art Institute of Chicago, IL, Alfred Stieglitz Collection
(1949.561), all rights reserved

ABOVE
John Marin
Ship, Sea and Sky Forms (An Impression), 1923
Watercolor, 13½ × 17 inches
Columbus Museum of Art, OH, gift of Ferdinand Howald (31.218)

RIGHT ABOVE
John Marin
Clouds and Mountains at Kufstein, 1910
Watercolor on paper, 15½ × 8⅝ inches
Courtesy of Museum of Fine Arts, Boston, MA, the Hayden
Collection, Charles Henry Hayden Fund (61.1139)

RIGHT BELOW
John Marin
Crotch Island, Maine, The Cove, 1924
Watercolor and black crayon on paper, 14⅜ × 17¼ inches
Courtesy of Museum of Fine Arts, Boston, MA, The Hayden
Collection, Charles Henry Hayden Fund (61.1140)

Charles Demuth
Irises, 1916
Watercolor on paper, 12⅞ × 7¹⁵⁄₁₆ inches
© The Cleveland Museum of Art, OH, Norman O. Stone and Ella A.
Stone Memorial Fund (53.323)

Charles Demuth
Peaches, 1923
Watercolor on paper, 11½ × 17½ inches
Philadelphia Museum of Art, PA, A. E. Gallatin Collection
(52.61.21)

LEFT ABOVE
Charles Demuth
Trees and Barns: Bermuda, 1917
Watercolor over graphite on paper, 10 × 14 inches
Williams College Museum of Art, Williamstown, MA, bequest of
Susan Watts Street (57.8)

LEFT BELOW
Charles Demuth
Red Poppies, 1929
Watercolor and pencil on paper, 13⅞ × 19¾ inches
The Metropolitan Museum of Art, New York, NY, gift of Henry
and Louise Loeb, 1983 (1983.40)

ABOVE
Charles Sheeler
Still Life and Shadows, 1924
Conté crayon, watercolor, and tempera on paper, 30¾ × 22⅞ inches
Columbus Museum of Art, OH, gift of Ferdinand Howald (31.106)

Charles Sheeler
River Rouge Industrial Plant, 1928
Graphite and watercolor on paper mounted on paper, 8⅜ × 11¼ inches
The Carnegie Museum of Art, gift of G. David Thompson
(57.12.7)

Lyonel Feininger
Strand, 1925
Watercolor and pen and ink on pulp paper, 11⁹⁄₁₆ × 17 inches
The Brooklyn Museum, NY, Museum Collection Fund (31.128)

Lyonel Feininger
The River, 1940
Ink and watercolor on paper, 11⅜ × 18³⁄₁₆ inches
Worcester Art Museum, Worcester, MA (1942.48)

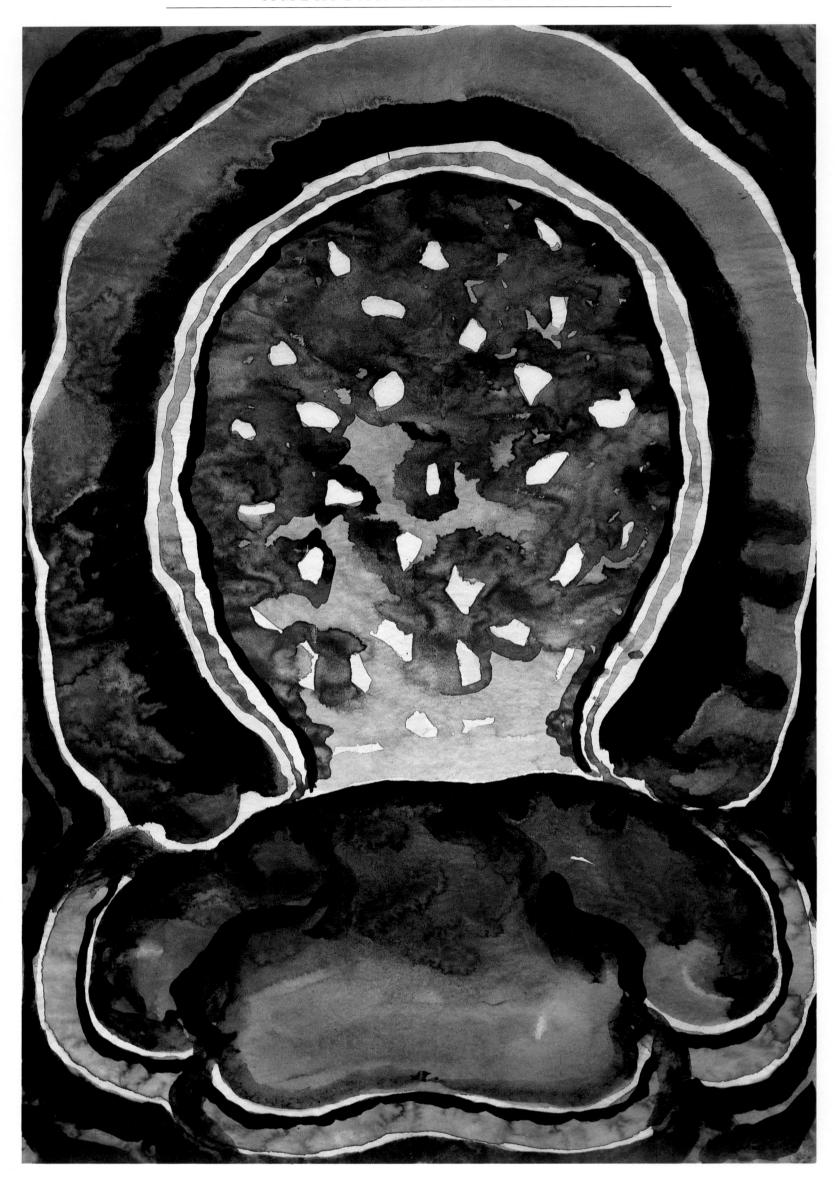

Georgia O'Keeffe
Abstraction, 1917
Watercolor, 15¾ × 10¾ inches
Collection of Mr and Mrs Gerald P. Peters, Santa Fe, NM

Georgia O'Keeffe
Pink and Green Mountains, 1917
Watercolor on paper, 8¹³⁄₁₆ × 11⅞ inches
Spencer Museum of Art, The University of Kansas, Laurence, KS (77.43)

Georgia O'Keeffe
*Red Canna, c.*1920
Watercolor on paper, 19⅜ × 13 inches
Yale University Art Gallery, New Haven, CT, gift of George
Hooper Fitch, BA 1932, and Mrs Fitch

Stuart Davis
Town Square, 1925-26
Watercolor on paper, 15⅜ × 22½ inches
The Newark Museum of Art, NJ, purchase 1930, The General Fund (30.74)
© 1995 Estate of Stuart Davis, Licensed by VAGA, New York, NY

Stuart Davis
Abstraction, 1937
Watercolor and gouache on paper, 17⅞ × 23⅜ inches
National Museum of American Art, Smithsonian Institution,
Washington, D.C., transfer from General Services
Administration (1972.81)/Art Resource, New York, NY
© 1995 Estate of Stuart Davis, Licensed by VAGA, New York, NY

Milton Avery
River in the Hills, 1940
Watercolor on paper, 30¾ × 22¼ inches
Courtesy of Museum of Fine Arts, Boston, MA, Hayden
Collection, Charles Henry Hayden Fund (1971.147)

Charles Burchfield
Lavendar and Old Lace, 1939-47
Watercolor on paper, 37 × 50 inches
From the Collection of the New Britain Museum of Art of
American Art, CT, Charles F. Smith Fund (1952-29)

Charles Burchfield
February Thaw, 1920
Watercolor over pencil on paper, 17⅞ × 27⅞ inches
The Brooklyn Museum, NY, John B. Woodward Memorial Fund (21.104)

Charles Burchfield
The Coming of Spring, 1917-43
Watercolor on paper mounted to presswood, 34 × 48 inches
The Metropolitan Museum of Art, New York, NY, George A. Hearn
Fund, 1943 (43.159.6)

100

Charles Burchfield
Overhanging Cloud in July, 1947-59
Watercolor on paper, 39½ × 35½ inches
Collection of Whitney Museum of American Art, New York,
purchase with funds from the Friends of the Museum (60.23)

101

CONTEMPORARY AND ABSTRACT WATERCOLORS

The dramatic changes evident in the style and composition of modern watercolors reflect the influence of two post-war movements in America, Surrealism and Abstract Expressionism. Traditional values of technical expertise and careful transcription of observed landscapes and figures were abandoned in favor of psychological exploration and dreamscapes of the imagination. A significant exhibition entitled 'Fantastic Art, Dada and Surrealism', held at the Museum of Modern Art in 1936, set the tone for a new spirit of adventure in all art media. The bizarre shapes and shifting, uncertain planes and atmosphere of painters such as Salvador Dali and Arshile Gorky were gradually adopted into the American watercolor idiom.

Mark Rothko's *Baptismal Scene* (1945) alludes to religious rites, yet its imagery is vague and distorted. Strange, biomorphic forms float together in a kind of underwater miasma, linked by spidery tendrils and spontaneous blots of color. These notations appear guided less by the artist's hand than by chance, effecting a collection of doodles that express a hallucinatory stream of consciousness.

Jackson Pollock took classes at the Art Students' League with the regionalist painter Thomas Hart Benton. On the advice of his psychiatrist, he began a series of compelling drawings and watercolors which was intended to parallel his intense emotions, and was used as a therapeutic device to resolve inner conflicts. There is an extraordinary linearity to automatic drawings such as *Untitled* in which frenzied skeins of marks, resembling scars, zippers, gashes, and even swastikas, fill the page with a tense energy like the violent aftermath of a nightmare.

The lush color and elegant calligraphy of Sam Francis' watercolors suggest the freedom and sun-drenched skies of his native California. Francis flicks drops of paint on to the page with a loaded brush, and when combined with his subtle, abstract arrangements of blots in vibrant, primary colors, they connote the lyricism of Chinese characters and scroll paintings.

David Levine is best known as a caricaturist and his finely-crafted image of a roller-coaster ride at Coney Island called *Atlantis* reveals his expert draftsmanship. It has the mood of an old newsreel, recording the amusements of an earlier era, and its details seem to fade and disperse into the horizon in blurring sepia tones, creating an elusive, otherworldly experience.

Claes Oldenburg is primarily a sculptor, and his watercolor sketches are an experimental forum for his humorous, colossal monuments to ordinary objects designed for public sites. His ironic commentaries on mass-produced icons of American culture, such as erasers, vacuum cleaners, toothpaste tubes, lipsticks and scissors, possess the kitsch appeal of the Pop artists of the 1960s. His absurd proposal for a clothes pin monument in Chicago is loosely rendered with fluid washes, and depends for its effect upon the viewer's awareness of the gag. In its distorted scale, the piece has an anthropomorphic flavor, like a circus hawkster on stilts presiding over a captive audience.

William Wiley's weird vision of an atelier gone awry in *Nothing Conforms* absorbs the Surrealist vernacular in its melting symbols of an artist's paraphernalia. Blotches of watercolor seep from discarded paint tubes; cobwebs collect in corners of frames, which in turn act as windows into other studios where blank canvases await; a melting candle sheds light on a ghostly skull; and, as the caption reads 'nothing conforms to x speck stations.' It is a complex, personal fantasy imbued with the highly idiosyncratic flavor of contemporary life.

The unfinished glimpse of a face in Chuck Close's *Study of Kent* is like a photograph being developed; Close's watercolors are related to the photorealist movement without its glamorous, glossy inventions. They borrow the technological processes of commercial printing, where layers of transparent colors are laid over one another to create the finished picture. Close's systematic dedication to the elements of vision, and his application of closely aligned dots in varying hues, is akin to the careful character studies of Thomas Eakins as well as to the strategies of the Pointillists. His lack of interest in pictorial prettiness or value judgments related to his sitters' features, however, and the changes in scale and presentation he employs, confirm a cool, modern detachment in his work, like the distant, arbitrary lens of the medium of television.

William T. Wiley
Nothing Conforms, 1978
Watercolor on paper, 29½ × 22½ inches
Collection of Whitney Museum of American Art, New York,
purchase with funds from the Neysa McMein Purchase Award
(79.25)

NOTHING CONFORMS TO X SPECK STATIONS .. FANCY REAM ARCES AND A LIL FALTER PEACE WHILE WAITING FOR THE MODEL ..
SHADOWSLICKASEALSLITHERTHROUGH

Sam Francis
Yellow, Violet and White Forms,
1956
Watercolor, 22⁷⁄₁₆ × 30³⁄₈
inches
The Brooklyn Museum, NY,
Dick S. Ramsay Fund (57.70)

Sam Francis
*Untitled, c.*1957
Watercolor on paper, 24¹⁄₁₆ × 19½ inches
Hirshhorn Museum and Sculpture Garden, Smithsonian Institution,
Washington, D.C., gift of Joseph H. Hirshhorn, 1966 (66.1931)

Jackson Pollock
Pattern, c.1945
Watercolor, brush and ink, pen and ink and gouache on paper,
22½ × 5½ inches (irregular)
Hirshhorn Museum and Sculpture Garden, Smithsonian
Institution, Washington, D.C., gift of the Joseph H. Hirshhorn
Foundation, 1966 (66.4086)

ABOVE
Jackson Pollock
Untitled, 1944
Pen and brush with black and colored ink on ivory wove paper,
18¾ × 24⅝ inches
© 1994 The Art Institute of Chicago, gift of Margaret Fisher, William
Hartmann, Joseph R. Shapiro, and Mrs Leigh B. Block;
Ada Turnbull Hertle Fund, 1966.350, all rights reserved

RIGHT
Mark Rothko
Baptismal Scene, 1945
Watercolor on paper, 19⅞ × 14 inches
Collection of Whitney Museum of American Art, New York,
purchase (46.12)

Acknowledgments

The publisher wishes to thank designer David Eldred, picture researcher Sara E Dunphy, production manager Simon Shelmerdine and editor Jessica Hodge. We should also like to thank the following institutions, agencies and individuals for permission to reproduce photographic material.

Allen Memorial Art Museum, Oberlin, OH: page 104

Art Resource, New York, NY: pages 33, 51

Art Institute of Chicago, IL: pages 57, 79, 83 bottom, 110

Brompton Picture Library: page 12 bottom

The Brooklyn Museum, NY: pages 8 (top), 32, 53, 54, 64 top, 65, 66/67, 72/73, 91 top, 99, 105, 106/107

Bowdoin College of Museum of Art, Brunswick, Maine: pages 10 bottom, 14

Carnegie Museum of Art, Pittsburg, PA: page 90

Cleveland Musum of Art, Cleveland, OH: page 86

Collection of the Charles Burchfield Archives, Burchfield Art Center, State University College at Buffalo, NY: page 21

Collection of the J Paul Getty Museum, Malibu, CA: page 18

Collection of the New York Historical Society, New York, NY: pages 7, 25 top, 26

Collection of Mr and Mrs Gerald P Peters, Santa Fe, NM: page 92

Columbus Museum of Art, Columbus, OH: pages 84, 89

Currier Gallery of Art, Manchester, NH: page 13

Delaware Art Museum, Wilmington, DE: page 22

Des Moines Art Center Permanent Collection, IA: page 23

Fine Arts Museum of San Francisco: page 9

Freer Gallery of Art, Smithsonian Institution, Washington, DC: pages 11, 39 both, 40

Harvard University Art Museums, Cambridge, MA: pages 41, 60/61, 74/75

Hirshhorn Museum and Sculpture Garden, Smithsonian Institution, Washington, DC: pages 2, 8 bottom (Charles Archival Collection), 108, 109

Isabella Stewart Gardner Museum, Boston, MA: page 69

The Metropolitan Museum of Art, New York, NY: pages 6, 17, 25 bottom, 27 top (photograph by Geoffrey Clements), 29 bottom (photograph by Geoffrey Clements), 34, 36, 37 (photograph by Geoffrey Clements), 42, 48, 49, 53, 55, 63, 81, 88 bottom, 100

Museum of Art, Rhode Island School of Design, Providence, RI: page 35 (photograph Cathy Carver)

Museum of Fine Arts, Boston, MA: pages 1, 10 top, 12 top, 19, 27 bottom, 28, 29 top, 30-31, 43, 44, 45, 46, 47, 50, 52, 58/59, 68, 70, 71, 80, 85 both, 97

National Academy of Design, New York: page 16

National Museum of American Art, Smithsonian Institution, Washington, D.C.: page 96

National Portrait Gallery, Smithsonian Institution, Washington, D.C.: page 15

New Britain Museum of American Art, CT: page 98

The Newark Museum of Art, Newark, NH: page 95

Philadelphia Museum of Art, PA: pages 83 top, 87

Spencer Museum of Art, University of Kansas, Lawrence, KS: page 93

Whitney Museum of American Art, New York, NY: pages 101 (photograph by Geoffrey Clements), 103 (photograph by Gemma One Conversions), 111 (photograph by Geoffrey Clements)

William A Farnsworth Library and Art Museum, Rockland, ME: pages 76/77, 78

Williams College Museum of Art, Williamstown, MA: page 88 top

Worcester Art Museum, Worcester, MA: pages 4/5, 64 bottom, 91 bottom

Yale University Art Gallery, New Haven, CT: pages 62, 94